THE UNTAMED WORLD

Japanese Macaques

Pat Miller-Schroeder

RAINTREE
STECK-VAUGHN
PUBLISHERS

A Harcourt Company

Austin   New York
www.raintreesteckvaughn.com

Published by Raintree Steck-Vaughn Publishers, an imprint of Steck-Vaughn Company.

Library of Congress Cataloging-in-Publication Data

Miller-Schroeder, Patricia.
    Japanese macaques/Pat Miller-Schroeder.
    p. cm. -- (The Untamed world)
    Includes bibliographical references (p.).
    ISBN 0-8172-4576-6
    1. Japanese macaque--Juvenile literature. [1. Japanese macaque. 2. Monkeys.] I. Title.
II. Series

    QL737.P93 M55 2001
    599.8'644--dc21

                                                                    2001019208

Printed and bound in Canada
1234567890 05 04 03 02 01

Project Coordinator
Heather Kissock
Editor
Lauri Seidlitz
Raintree Steck-Vaughn Editor
Pam Wells
Copy Editor
Jennifer Nault
Design and Illustration
Warren Clark
Layout
Terry Paulhus

Consultants
James Paterson, University of Calgary, Department of Anthropology
Mary Pavelka, University of Calgary, Department of Anthropology
David Sprague, University of Tsukuba, Institute of History and Anthropology

Acknowledgments
The publisher wishes to thank Warren Rylands for inspiring this series.

Photograph Credits

Corel Corporation: page 45; **Ivy Images:** pages 5 (Duane Sept), 11 (Tony Makepeace), 13 (Bill Ivy), 16 (Steve Kaufmann), 27 (Duane Sept), 31 (Duane Sept), 60 (Steve Kaufmann); **David Jack:** pages 6, 17, 18, 23, 24, 25, 26, 42, 54; **Steve Kaufmann:** pages 4, 14, 19, 22, 29, 30, 32, 36, 37, 40, 41, 43, 44, 53, 59; **James Paterson:** pages 20, 21, 55, 57; **Tom Stack & Associates:** pages 10 (Dominique Brand), 28 (G. Milburn); **J.D. Taylor:** pages 7, 9, 12, 15, 61; **Visuals Unlimited:** cover (Fritz Pölking), page 33 (Fritz Pölking).

Contents

Introduction 5

Features 7

Social Life 15

Young 23

Habitat 31

Food 37

Competition 41

Folklore 47

Status 53

Twenty Fascinating Facts 59

Glossary 62

Suggested Reading 63

Index 64

Introduction

The Japanese macaque lives farther north than any other nonhuman primate.

Opposite: The Japanese macaque is well known in the stories and legends of Japan, where it has lived for thousands of years.

On the faraway islands of Japan lives a wonderfully unique monkey. The Japanese macaque (muh-KAHK) lives farther north than any other nonhuman **primate**. Some groups of Japanese macaques even live in areas that have a few months of winter each year. These macaques are sometimes called "snow monkeys."

What is the Japanese macaque really like? Come now and visit the world of these fascinating creatures. You will discover how the monkeys can survive an icy winter storm. You will be amazed at the way many of them have learned to swim and dive in the sea. You will see what happens when a troublesome group of monkeys is sent to live in the wilds of Texas. So read on to enter the wild and wonderful world of the Japanese macaque.

The name "snow monkey" is misleading since most Japanese macaques live in subtropical climates.

Features

Like other primates, Japanese macaques are tough, clever, and learn quickly in new situations.

Japanese macaques are able to live in many types of habitats because they are **adaptable**. This is a feature they share with other monkeys and apes. Some macaques have special adaptations to cold weather. Others have adaptations for life on a seaside beach or a mountain forest. Their flexibility has even allowed some of them to live in a hot, dry, desert environment. Like other primates, Japanese macaques are tough, clever, and learn quickly in new situations.

Opposite: Japanese macaques are at home in a variety of habitats.

These monkeys learn quickly, and new skills are passed from one group to another.

Classification

Japanese macaques belong to a large order of animals called primates. Primates include monkeys, apes, and prosimians, which are animals such as lemurs and lorises. Humans are also primates.

Scientists do not agree on exactly how many species of primates there are today. The number is probably around 180 species. The smallest primate is the tiny mouse lemur that weighs only 2 ounces (60 g). The mighty gorilla is the largest, at about 400 pounds (180 kg). Japanese macaques, at around 28 pounds (13 kg), are somewhere in the middle.

Japanese macaques are most closely related to 15 other species of macaques. Macaques are all medium-sized, stocky monkeys. Their arms and legs are nearly equal in length, and they walk on all fours. All macaques are at home both in the trees and on the ground.

MACAQUE SPECIES

Macaques are found in Morocco, Algeria, Gibraltar, Afghanistan, India, China, Japan, and other places in southeast Asia, including the Philippines, Borneo, Sumatra, Java, and Sulawesi.

Common Name	Latin Name
Barbary macaque	Macaca sylvanus
Lion-tailed macaque	Macaca silenus
Moor macaque	Macaca maura
Pigtailed macaque	Macaca nemestrina
Sulawesi booted macaque	Macaca ochreata
Sulawesi crested macaque	Macaca nigra
Tonken macaque	Macaca tonkeana
Crab-eating macaque	Macaca fascicularis
Japanese macaque	Macaca fuscata
Rhesus macaque	Macaca mulatta
Taiwanese macaque	Macaca cyclopis
Toque macaque	Macaca sinica
Assamese macaque	Macaca assamensis
Bonnet macaque	Macaca radiata
Tibetan stump-tailed macaque	Macaca thibetana
Bear macaque	Macaca arctoides

Size

Japanese macaques are about the size of a cocker spaniel. When full grown, males are slightly larger than females. Their weight varies from 20 to 40 pounds (9 to 18 kg). The average weight of males is 32 pounds (14.6 kg). For females the average weight is 27 pounds (12.3 kg). Average height is about 2 feet (60 cm) from head to rump. Males can look even larger because they have more muscles and hair on their shoulders and hips. The largest Japanese macaques live in the coldest part of their range in Japan's snow-covered mountains.

LIFE SPAN

Japanese macaques can live between 25 and 30 years. One hazard some wild macaques face is severe winter weather, resulting in food shortages. Other monkeys may die from injuries or illnesses such as pneumonia. There are few natural predators in their habitat.

There may be several ages and sizes of macaques in a group. Newborns weigh only 1 pound (0.45 kg). They grow to 4 pounds (2 kg) by 4 months and reach 20 to 40 pounds (9 to 18 kg) as adults.

Life in the Cold

Japanese macaques that live in colder regions have developed special habits that help them survive. These snow monkeys live through a cold winter by using every bit of available food. They strip the bark from tree branches and twigs. They also search for and eat the trees' tightly curled winter buds and shoots.

Some macaques keep warm by soaking in naturally occurring hot springs. There are many of these springs scattered in the mountains. The monkeys sit up to their necks in the steaming water that may have a temperature of up to 109° F (43° C). When they get out of the warm pools, they depend on their long coats of fur and quick movement to keep them warm.

The macaques sometimes fluff out their fur, trapping air pockets to keep in body heat. Whole family groups sleep huddled closely together for warmth at night.

Over many centuries Japanese macaques have adapted to life in the cold. In Japan's mountain forests, the temperature regularly falls to 5° F (-15° C) for part of the year.

Fur and Skin

Japanese macaque fur varies in color and length depending on where they live. The monkeys living in the coldest regions have long, gray-colored coats. Those in the warmer parts of their range have short, brown hair. One group of macaques that lives on a small island has a greenish tinge to its fur. In cold areas, the heavy winter coat is shed in the spring. When the cold weather returns in the fall, the heavy fur grows back. Male Japanese macaques often grow a longer cape of fur on their shoulders during the mating season. Young macaques usually have dark brown or black fur, while the fur of old animals is often gray.

Japanese macaques are sometimes called red-faced macaques. They are called this because the pink skin on their faces and rumps changes to a deep red during the breeding season. Old macaques sometimes have blotchy faces.

Japanese macaques have special pads of hard skin on their rumps. These pads make it more comfortable to sit for long periods of time on hard surfaces. This feature is important because many macaques sleep sitting up in trees.

Rump pads help cushion hard surfaces on the ground and in the trees.

Special Adaptations

Japanese macaques have other special adaptations that help them live successfully in their many types of habitats.

Hands and Feet

Japanese macaque hands are very much like yours and mine. They have four flexible fingers and an **opposable** thumb. This lets them pinch their fingers and thumb together to grasp things. Having hands that can grasp allows macaques to firmly hang on to objects, such as branches, which is important for climbing safely on trees. Macaques have tiny, raised ridges on their fingertips that help them feel and grip objects. Their fingers also help them keep their fur clean.

Like most primates, Japanese macaque feet are like their hands. Their feet are flat with five toes. The big toes are opposable like their thumbs. This allows macaques to hold objects with their feet. This is a big help when they climb or cling to a branch. Infant macaques use their feet to help them cling securely to their mother's fur.

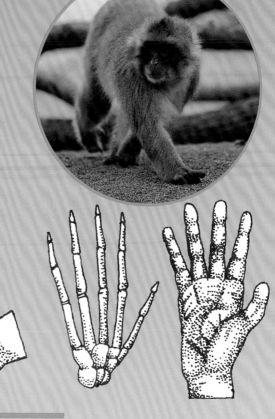

Opposable thumbs allow macaques to pick up small objects such as seeds. This makes feeding on a variety of food easier.

Movement

Japanese macaques walk on all four limbs like a dog, with the palms of their hands and feet touching down flat on the ground. Macaques are not limited to the ground, however. They can travel, sit, and feed in trees high above the ground. In some areas, macaques have also learned to swim and dive.

Sight, Smell, and Hearing

Sight is the most important sense to monkeys such as Japanese macaques. They have two large, forward-facing eyes. They can judge distance and depth while moving and can sharply focus on movement around them. Like humans, macaques see in color. This lets them use color cues in finding and identifying food.

Japanese macaques have flat faces and small noses. Their nostrils are set close together and are turned downwards. Their sense of smell helps macaques find food and gives them other information about their environment. Still, their sense of smell is not nearly as important as their vision.

Macaque ears are small and set close to their head. They do not move around like the ears of animals such as rabbits. However, the sense of hearing is important to macaques. It helps them communicate when they travel through the forest. It helps them detect danger and warn

Male macaques have very large canine teeth. These are for defense and for showdowns with other males.

one another. When a sound is heard, the macaques normally use their sense of sight to help them locate its source.

Teeth and Cheek Pouches

An adult macaque has 32 teeth just like an adult human. They have teeth for biting and slicing and teeth for grinding and crushing. They are able to eat a wide variety of different foods with these teeth.

Macaques have large pouches inside their cheeks. These expand and can be packed full of food such as fruits or grains. This allows the monkeys to quickly gather a lot of food.

canines

Social Life

There is safety in numbers because the troop provides protection from predators.

Opposite: Each troop has its favorite feeding spots to visit.

Japanese macaques live in social groups called troops. The troop is very important to these monkeys. When they are young, the troop gives them a safe, secure place in which to grow. There is safety in numbers because the troop provides protection from predators. Food may be easier to find in a troop since each troop has its own favorite feeding spots.

Female Japanese macaques spend their whole life in their original troop. Most male Japanese macaques move from one troop to another when they mature. Many change troops several times. Some become wanderers, joining a troop only during the breeding season.

Social life means following the rules of social behavior whether in a wild or captive group.

Troop Composition

Troops of Japanese macaques usually contain 20 to 100 animals. In areas where the monkeys are **provisioned**, or food is supplied, troops of 500 to 1,000 animals have been reported. If a troop becomes too large, it may break into two smaller troops.

The troop is organized around groups of closely related female monkeys. A group like this is called a **matriline**. A matriline may contain mothers, daughters, grandmothers, granddaughters, aunts, nieces, female cousins, and sisters. Each matriline has certain males that it favors. These males are usually not related to the females. When they mature, most males leave their original troop. The few that stay keep close ties to their mothers and sisters.

There are almost always more adult females than adult males in a troop. Each troop also has several infants and juvenile members. Most troops have one top male and one top female. They are called the alpha male and the alpha female. The alpha male needs the alpha female's support to keep his position in the troop.

A troop is a safe, secure place in which to grow up. Most young are surrounded by relatives.

Each troop has leaders who keep a careful watch for both danger and problems within the group.

Life in the Troop

Life in the troop is usually orderly. Everyone has their special place based on whom they are related to or who their friends are. If disputes break out, monkeys depend on family or friends to support them. Matrilines are maintained because female relatives support one another.

There are separate **dominance hierarchies** for males and females. The alpha males are the highest ranking males. They stay in the central part of the troop with the most dominant female matrilines. Males who are getting ready to leave the troop live on its outer edges. Males who are trying to join the troop live here as well. These monkeys are called **peripheral males** and are usually low ranking. Low-ranking females sometimes develop special friendships with these males.

The top-ranking male leader is in charge of protecting the troop. The top-ranking female leads the troop. Both alpha males and alpha females settle disputes between troop members.

Grooming

Grooming is an important activity in the Japanese macaque troop. It brings troop members together in a pleasant social activity. Most grooming occurs between mothers and their offspring. There is also grooming between adults, but adult males rarely groom one another.

During grooming, a monkey lies flat on its belly or side in front of another monkey. It may also sit with its head down or its body bent backward. Its position depends on where it wants to be groomed. The other monkey parts its hair in layers and picks out things such as bugs, leaves, scabs, and dandruff. The grooming monkey usually eats these tidbits.

Japanese macaques do not pant or sweat very much. Grooming helps keep them comfortable by letting air reach their skin.

Grooming is a social glue. It helps to keep the group together.

Play

Play is also an important part of life in the macaque troop. Young Japanese macaques spend a great deal of time playing. Play allows them to test their strength and skills. It also teaches them about macaque social behavior. When youngsters wrestle and chase each other, they have fun. They also work out their place in the troop's social hierarchy.

Young macaques form play groups, and both males and females play rough-and-tumble games. If play gets too rough, mothers or older siblings will rescue the youngsters. As juvenile macaques grow, males go off with playmates for longer periods of time. Females stay closer to their female relatives. They may begin to "play mother" to other infants. This means they will try to hold and carry infants and practice being mothers. Both male and female adult macaques will sometimes play with infants or juveniles. Juvenile males especially like to play with and be around adult males.

Play is an important activity for learning the behaviors and skills needed to live in the troop.

Communication

Japanese macaques are very intelligent animals that have many different ways of communicating. They use different **vocalizations**, body language, and displays to send messages to one another.

Vocalizations

Monkeys are usually noisy creatures, and Japanese macaques are no exception. Their vocabulary includes more than 30 types of sounds. These include a variety of whistles, warbles, squawks, squeals, growls, and screeches. These calls are ways of showing such emotions as fear, sorrow, anger, pleasure, or affection.

They have special warning cries to alert others of predators or other dangers. Japanese macaques that have been moved to a colony in Texas have created a special warning call for rattlesnakes. This call is only used for this danger. The monkeys had never seen a rattlesnake before coming to Texas. Researchers studying these monkeys have learned to recognize the rattlesnake warning call. It has saved at least one scientist from being bitten by a snake.

Vocal messages let macaques show how they are feeling. The messages can include warnings and invitations.

Body Language

Vocalizations are often combined with body language to send messages. Body language includes facial expressions or the way an animal moves its body. For example, if one monkey stares at another, it is a threat. If the monkey wants to look even more threatening, it lowers its head, wrinkles its forehead, raises its eyebrows, and flattens its ears and head hair. It will then thrust out its mouth and make sharp, puffing sounds. The more parts of this threat display that are used, the bigger the warning to the other animal. The monkey is saying, "Back off or else!"

A monkey receiving a threat or who is tense about something makes a "fear grimace." It may also return the threat by raising its eyebrows or dropping its lower jaw in a "gape." Monkeys who want to do something friendly, like grooming, will smack their lips. When animals want to play or are playing, they use a special "play face." In this signal the mouth is wide open, and both top and bottom teeth show what looks like a grin. This is only a little of the rich body language used by macaques.

Displays

Japanese macaques have a special display that they use to announce their presence to other macaques. It is called the long-distance tree display. The full display involves swaying and shaking the tops of evergreen trees. A roaring vocalization is given at the same time. This display is usually given between males of neighboring troops. It can also be given by wandering males when they approach a strange troop during the breeding season. High-ranking females may give the tree shaking display but do not roar warnings.

Body language can be read by all members of the group.

Young

Most of the members of a nursing group are related.

Opposite: There is a close bond between mother and infant macaques.

When a Japanese macaque infant is born, it is the focus of interest for other troop members. Females and juveniles try to look at it and touch it. The newborn's mother is very protective. She will not let others get too close. It is not long, however, before the infant becomes an active, playful member of the troop. Mother and infant become part of a nursing group with other mothers and infants. Most members of a nursing group are related. It is a safe place for the infant to grow and explore its new world.

With their mothers and other relatives close by, young macaques have a secure place to explore their world.

Breeding Seasons

Japanese macaques breed in the fall or early winter. This is to make sure that infants are not born in the cold winter months. Breeding seasons vary depending on where the troop lives. In the southern part of Japan, the monkey breeding season is from November to February. In the north it lasts only from October to December.

When the breeding season occurs, Japanese macaques' faces flush a bright red. This is because of **hormones** that are released in their bodies at this time. Both females and males mate with many partners during the breeding season. Young are born the following spring or early summer.

A female's face also flushes bright red when she is pregnant or nursing an infant.

Birth

Gestation time for Japanese macaques is about six months. Most infants are born from mid-April to mid-July. When the mother is ready to give birth, she becomes restless and looks for a secluded spot. One of her female relatives may stay close by while she gives birth.

Japanese macaques are almost always born at night. It is safest to give birth while the troop is resting. That way the mother will not be left behind while the troop moves during the day in search of food.

A female first gives birth when she is about 5 years old. She is not even fully grown at this time. The oldest recorded female to give birth was 25 years old. Females usually give birth to one infant at a time. Twins are rarely born. Females give birth every one and one-half to three years.

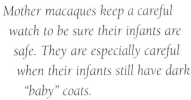

Mother macaques keep a careful watch to be sure their infants are safe. They are especially careful when their infants still have dark "baby" coats.

Infants

Newborn macaques are tiny and helpless. Soft, dark, baby fur covers their bodies. Their spindly arms and legs are pencil thin. Big eyes stare out of tiny, wrinkled faces. Even though they look weak, infant macaques can cling to their mother's fur with their hands and feet. Shortly after birth, the infant begins feeding on its mother's milk. The mother cradles and supports her infant as it nurses.

Infants depend totally on their mother's milk for the first three months. They will still nurse for several months after this if their mother lets them.

Care of Young

The mother provides all of the care for the infant at first. Mother and baby must travel with the troop. The infant clings to the fur on its mother's chest or belly as she walks on all fours. For the first few hours after birth, the mother walks on three legs and supports the infant with one hand. She grooms it during rest times and keeps it warm and safe. After these first hours, the infant must be able to hold on itself.

The newborn macaque depends on its mother's milk for the first three months. The mother teaches the youngster what is good to eat and what is harmful. She encourages its attempts to walk and climb. She supervises its first attempts to play with other infants and comes to its aid whenever it calls for help. Mothers restrain adventurous infants by holding them by one foot and staring at them.

Other members of the troop help care for the infant as it grows. Adult females and juvenile males and females groom it and keep it from wandering. Its older brothers and sisters pay special attention to it. Infants can survive without their mothers as early as three months if another troop member adopts it. Males have been known to adopt older infants or yearlings that need attention. Males sometimes comfort, carry, protect, or play with young macaques. Others will have little to do with the young ones. On the whole, the troop provides many caregivers who are willing to give young macaques attention and support.

Infant macaques are a focus for attention. Many caregivers in the troop take time to groom them.

Development

1 to 3 Months

Newborn macaques weigh less than 1 pound (0.45 kg). Their tiny bodies measure only 4 inches (10 cm) long, and their fur is dark brown or black. Nursing is their main source of food, but they begin tasting solid food as early as 2 weeks. They hold on to their mother's fur with their hands and feet. They ride clinging to their mother's belly at first. They can sit up and move around by 1 week and walk on all fours by 3 weeks. They begin to play with other infants in their nursing group.

3 to 6 Months

The growing infant sheds its dark baby coat by 3 months. By 4 months they are chubby and furry, weighing about 4 pounds (2 kg). They now ride on their mother's back jockey style. By 3 months they begin foraging for food with their mothers. They learn to stuff their cheek pouches. Most still nurse and come to mothers for comfort and protection.

Young macaques often hitch a ride on their mothers. They cling securely with both hands and feet.

Play is an important part of macaque development. Play groups let older youngsters practice social skills.

6 Months to 1 Year

Males and females begin to behave differently by 6 months. Females spend more time close to their mothers and other female relatives. Males spend more time with playmates in play groups away from their mothers. Both males and females forage for food on their own and eat everything adults do. Mothers often prevent them from nursing.

1 to 2 Years

The young macaques are completely **weaned**. Males continue to spend more time away from mothers. Their play is very boisterous, and they are interested in adult males. Females show a growing interest in infants. They try play-mothering. Young males are sometimes adopted by adult males. Both males and females like to swim and play in water.

2 to 3 Years

Juvenile males spend most of their time in peer groups and associate with the peripheral males. Females become more involved with play-mothering and practice caring for infants. Females sometimes try new foods or behaviors that other troop members adopt.

3 to 7 Years

Males spend their time on the periphery of the troop. Some leave the troop for long periods. Eventually they stay away and wander alone or in small, all-male groups. Most eventually join a new troop. At 4 to 5 years, females mate for the first time. Most become mothers at about 5 years. Males can mate at 6 years but will not be full size until they are 8 years old.

Habitat

Japanese macaques have adapted to a wide variety of climates.

Opposite: Japan's mountain forests provide a challenging environment for the macaques that live there.

Macaques that live in the southern parts of Japan enjoy warmer temperatures and a wider variety of food.

Japanese macaques live on most of the islands of Japan. They have adapted to a wide variety of climates. Much of their natural habitat lies in the mountain forests that once covered much of Japan. In the northern part of their range, snow blankets the ground from December to March. Snowdrifts are up to 13 feet (4 m) deep and cover most of the vegetation. Trees lose their leaves and temperatures drop to 5° F (-15° C). Some macaques live at elevations higher than 9,600 feet (2,926 m) above sea level.

Japanese macaques also live on the southern islands of Japan. Here snow is not often seen, and most of the trees keep their leaves year round. Some live in coastal areas. Here they forage for food on the beaches and swim in the sea.

Home Range

The **home ranges** of Japanese macaques vary in size depending on how much food there is to eat. Groups that live in the warmer south have no need for large home ranges. Food is plentiful year round. Here home ranges may be as small as 0.4 square miles (1 sq km). The average range in the south is 2 square miles (5 sq km). In the north where food is scarce for part of the year, home ranges may be 7 to 11 square miles (20 to 30 sq km).

Japanese macaques' home ranges are being upset by forest clearing in many areas. If this happens the macaques must search an even larger area for food. They may have to cover 14 square miles (36 sq km) or more.

Troops' home ranges sometimes overlap. Most of the time, neighboring troops avoid each other. They let each other know where they are by shaking treetops. If they do meet, encounters are most often quiet, but fighting can occur.

Each troop has its own home range where it lives and searches for food. Where food is scarce, home ranges are large.

Seasonal Activities

Japanese macaques are affected a great deal by the seasons. The monkeys must depend on different foods in different seasons. The troop travels to various parts of their home range depending on where the best food can be found at that time of year. Spring and fall are times of plenty. Food is available in many parts of the range.

In the cold winter months, northern macaques spend less time traveling. It takes a lot of energy to plow through snowdrifts. During the cold season, snow monkeys will often sleep huddled together for warmth. They can form huge furry balls, with little faces peaking out of the fur. Groups of three or four monkeys have been seen lined up on tree branches, hugging each other front to back.

In winter Japanese macaques grow thick fur and huddle together to share their body heat.

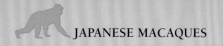

Viewpoints

Should problem macaque troops be sent to other countries?

The Japanese macaque is quickly running out of living space. Its habitat is disappearing, and many macaques are being killed or trapped as crop-raiding pests every year. Twenty-five years ago a pest troop was successfully relocated to the United States. There it has grown and thrived. It provides opportunities to study semiwild macaques in a new environment. Is living as a refugee the only hope for the Japanese macaque?

PRO

1 Setting up colonies of Japanese macaques in other countries gives students in these countries a chance to study semiwild primates. Otherwise, many students have to travel great distances for this opportunity.

2 Many of these pest troops would be destroyed if they were not relocated. Moving them saves their lives.

3 Japanese macaques are a treasure for all the world's people. Every country has a duty to save them.

CON

1 Students of primate behavior can learn the most about Japanese macaques by studying them in their own habitat.

2 Capturing and transporting pest troops can cause death and injury to some troop members.

3 Moving macaques does not solve the problem of their shrinking habitat.

Primate Researchers Talk About Japanese Macaques

Mary McDonald Pavelka

"On one occasion a monkey 'saved' me from stepping on a rattlesnake that was lying in the grass just a few feet ahead of me. She was sitting in a nearby bush and gave the call, and I stopped walking even before I was aware of what I had heard."

Mary McDonald Pavelka began studying the Japanese macaques of the Arashiyama West troop in Dilley, Texas, in 1981. She now teaches primatology at the University of Calgary in Canada. She and her students continue to study the Arashiyama West troop, making many fascinating discoveries. Dr. Pavelka has written a book, *Monkeys of the Mesquite*, about her work with the Texas snow monkeys.

David Sprague

"Many monkey populations are pests, partly because habitat destruction deprived them of natural foods. The pest populations may be the only monkey populations actually present in much of the country."

David Sprague has been studying the wild Japanese macaques on Yakushima Island for the past ten years. He teaches at the University of Kyoto and coedits the "Japan Primate Newsletter." He is involved with saving the remaining wild Japanese macaques and their habitat.

Linda Fedigan

"A primate mother is much more than a warm body...and a milk supply. She is also the infant's introduction into the complex social world in which it must survive. Her behavior sets the stage upon which her offspring's social life drama will unfold."

Linda Fedigan began studying Japanese macaques in 1971 when the Arashiyama West troop was moved from Japan to Texas. She lived with the troop for more than three years. Dr. Fedigan teaches primatology at the University of Alberta and in Texas. She has edited and written many books and articles on Japanese macaques and other primates.

Food

The macaques' natural habitat provides them with a wide variety of foods.

Opposite: Japanese macaques are not fussy eaters. They eat most parts of plants including tree bark.

Japanese macaques are **omnivores**, which means they eat both plants and animals. Their natural habitat provides them with a wide variety of foods. Their favorite foods seem to be fruits, berries, acorns, and nuts. However, they also eat leaves, grasses, seeds, flowers, green stalks, and fruit pits. In winter, many live on only tree bark and the winter buds and sprouts of trees. In some areas they eat algae and kelp that wash onto beaches.

The macaques' habitat also provides them with a variety of animal foods. They eat spiders, insects, larvae, snails, crabs, crayfish, and barnacles. Some take eggs from birds' nests.

Fungi such as mushrooms also provide food. On one small island, there are no fruits, nuts, or leaves for part of the year. Macaques living on that island eat more than 20 kinds of fungus.

Most Japanese macaques are willing to try new foods. They learn the best way to handle unfamiliar food by trial and error and by watching each other.

Food Preparation

Japanese macaques are clever animals. This shows in the way they learn to eat and handle new foods. The most famous example of this cleverness was observed in a troop on Koshima Island. Japanese scientists had started putting out food on the beaches for the macaques. They wanted to bring them out in the open to study them. They put out food such as sweet potatoes and wheat. Soon the macaques regularly visited the beach.

The macaques liked the food on the beach, but it was often coated with sand. One young female called Imo started washing her sweet potatoes in a pool of water. Soon other young monkeys learned to do this by watching her. Eventually most of the monkeys in the troop were washing their sweet potatoes. That happened more than 40 years ago. Today even infants in that troop wash their food. Imo later switched to washing her sweet potatoes in the sea. Perhaps she liked the taste of salt. The other macaques again followed her example.

fruits
berries
nuts

Japanese macaques eat a variety of food.

crabs
insects
snails

Japanese Macaques: True or False?

Try this quiz to see how much you know about macaques.
Are the following statements true or false?
The answers are at the bottom of this page.

1 Japanese macaques break twigs and small branches and drop bits of food and vegetation while feeding. This provides food for small creatures such as ants or beetles.

2 Japanese macaques sleep in trees because they have many natural enemies that live on the ground.

3 Macaques provide a home for parasites such as tapeworms. Insects, such as flies or lice, may live in their fur.

4 Undigested seeds in monkey droppings spread seeds from one part of the habitat to another. This helps ensure a continuing food supply for themselves and others.

5 Japanese macaques depend on their sense of smell to locate food sources.

6 Japanese macaques have teeth that help them grind plant food and teeth that help them bite animal flesh.

7 Macaques are very choosy about what they will eat and depend upon a small number of food sources in their habitat.

8 Japanese macaques have pouches on their stomachs like kangaroos that help them store and carry food.

1) True.

2) False. Other than humans, Japanese macaques have few natural enemies.

3) True. Other monkeys may eat these insects while grooming.

4) False.

5) False. Macaques are more likely to use their sense of sight to find food.

6) True. Macaques, like humans, are omnivores.

7) False. Macaques are highly adaptable and will try and learn to eat new foods if they have the chance.

8) False. Japanese macaques have cheek pouches that help them carry food from one place to another.

Competition

Today humans are still the macaques' main competitors.

Opposite: Humans and macaques have a long history together. In some areas the monkeys go about their business close to admiring tourists.

Scientists who study fossils believe that macaques have lived in Japan for at least one to two million years. They probably came across a bridge of land that once connected Japan to the Asia mainland.

Descendants of these macaques spread out onto all of the Japanese islands except the most northern one, Hokkaido. There was plenty of food in the natural habitat. The troops did not have to compete if they spread out. There were not many predators to bother the macaques either. The one serious natural enemy of the macaques was the human, who hunted them for furs and food. Today humans are still the macaques' main competitors. They compete for shrinking habitat and kill them as crop-raiding pests.

Not all people admire the macaques. Crop-raiding macaques must keep a lookout for the many farmers who see them as pests.

Challenges from Other Japanese Macaques

Japanese macaques do not usually have to compete with one another for food. In their natural habitat, undisturbed by humans, there is enough for all. Troops avoid each other if possible. If troops meet, encounters can be peaceful, with some troops even traveling together for a while. Yet other encounters can be ferocious. Some studies show that matrilines and their male friends cooperate to fight troops over home ranges. In Yakushima researchers have seen some troops grow smaller and finally disappear as their home ranges shrank.

Males may compete for females in the breeding season. Wandering males visit other troops at this time hoping for the chance to breed. However, females choose their mating partners. Sometimes new males are welcomed, and sometimes they are chased away.

Life in the macaque troop is usually orderly. If disputes do occur, monkeys depend on family or friends to support them. The alpha male may settle disputes in the troop.

Relationships with Other Animals

Japanese macaques share their habitat with several other animals. Because of habitat destruction, many of these creatures are disappearing. The Asiatic black bear still lives in Japan, but its numbers are not large. Bears are omnivores like the macaques, but they do not seem to compete. The serow, a rare goat-antelope, lives in the mountain forests. In the winter the serow lives on twigs and branches like the macaques, but they do not compete either.

Other animals that macaques may encounter include the raccoon dog, red fox, pine marten, hare, badger, and flying squirrel. None of these animals interfere with the macaques. Eagles and large Ural owls may occasionally take a macaque infant. Packs of **feral** dogs sometimes hunt in the macaques' territories. However, Japanese macaques mostly go about their business undisturbed by the other creatures in their habitat.

The Japanese macaque shares its mountain forest home with other creatures, such as the rare serow.

Competing with Humans

Although Japanese macaques live peacefully with most other animals, they are often in competition with humans. Humans have hunted the monkeys for centuries. At first, they used primitive weapons, such as arrows and spears.

エサは絶対にやらないで下さい

Later, guns and traps were used. Some of the worst competition between humans and macaques has happened fairly recently.

A huge number of people live in the small area of the Japanese islands. People often see the forests as resources to be cut for lumber or cleared for farming. People want roads into the mountains and recreation sites in the macaques' forest home. As the macaques' habitat has shrunk, they have moved into human territory, raiding crops and entering towns. To many people in Japan, the monkeys have become pests.

There is a limited amount of space on the Japanese islands for both macaques and people. Even in remote areas, humans are now affecting the macaques' habitat.

Decline in Population

Japanese macaque populations are declining all over Japan. The worst problem facing Japanese macaques is the rapid loss of their habitat. For centuries Japanese forests have provided everything the macaques needed to survive. Now, increasing pressure from Japan's growing population is causing the monkeys' forest home to shrink. As forests are cut, new species of trees are being planted to take their place. These new trees often provide good lumber but no food for the macaques.

The Japanese cedar is a good tree for lumber but not for Japanese macaque food.

Folklore

The Japanese macaque has long been a part of Japanese folklore. In most tales the monkeys have been considered very wise. The famous symbol of the Three Wise Monkeys who "See No Evil, Hear No Evil, and Speak No Evil" is based on the Japanese macaque. Some people believe Japanese macaques bring good luck. Many visitors go to an ancient Buddhist monkey shrine at a place called Nara. Here, they touch an image of a smiling monkey in red robes, hoping it will bring them good luck. On the other hand, the name for "monkey" and "to go away" are both "saru." Gamblers and others who do not want to lose their luck will not say the monkey's name. They are afraid their luck will go away. In folklore, just as it is today, there are mixed feelings about Japan's monkeys.

Opposite: The three wise monkeys are named Mizaru, Kikazaru, and Iwazaru. These names mean "See No Evil," "Hear No Evil," and "Speak No Evil" in Japanese.

The Japanese macaque is a central figure in many of Japan's folk legends.

Folklore History

Japan's monkeys have long been thought to protect children and horses. Mothers sometimes give small monkey toys to children. Sometimes they even sew small monkey figures on their children's clothing to keep away evil spirits. At a famous temple, in a place called Nikko, there is a stable where royal horses were once kept. There are many carvings of monkeys above the stable doors to protect the horses from harm.

Monkeys are also honored in Japan by having every twelfth year named after them. Monkeys are believed to be one of the 12 animals that visited Buddha on his deathbed. Children who are born in the Year of the Monkey are believed to have the same traits the monkey has. These children are believed to be clever but emotional and not dependable. The next year of the monkey is in 2004.

Each birth year is named after one of the animals that came to see Buddha.

The Year of the…

Myths vs. Facts

Uttering a monkey's name can make good luck disappear. Touching a monkey statue can make good luck happen.

Monkeys have very little to do with people's luck.

Monkeys are clever tricksters who will harm you if you give them a chance.

Monkeys are clever, but they use their cleverness to find enough food to eat. They also use it to keep their troop safe.

Monkeys are dirty, messy animals. They smell bad and have no manners.

Monkeys spend a good deal of time grooming their fur to keep it clean. They smell no more than humans who wear no deodorant. Monkeys have a very clear set of "monkey manners" that they follow to keep life in the troop running smoothly.

Folktales

Japanese macaques appear in many old Japanese folktales. They often appear as clever tricksters who outsmart themselves. Sometimes a monkey trickster outsmarts others who want to take advantage of him. These stories provide lessons for people. Here are some Japanese folktales you may want to read for yourself. Your library is likely to have others.

Clever Monkeys

In "Raw Monkey Liver," a king tries to trick a monkey into visiting his castle so that he can get his sick daughter monkey liver to eat. The clever monkey finds out and escapes with his liver unharmed.

Bang, Garreth. *Men From the Village Deep In the Mountain and Other Folk Tales*. New York: MacMillan Publishing, 1973.

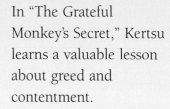

In "The Grateful Monkey's Secret," Kertsu learns a valuable lesson about greed and contentment.

Uchida, Yoshiko. Adapted from Saru no Ongaeshi. *The Sea of Gold and Other Tales from Japan*. Boston: Gregg Press, 1965.

Monkeys Learn a Lesson

In "Monkey and Crab," Monkey outwits Mother Crab and her children, stealing their food and hurting Mrs. Crab. However, he learns a lesson at the hands of the crab children and their friends.

Kawashima Watkins, Yoko. *Tales From the Bamboo Grove*. New York: Bradbury Press, 1992.

In "The Terrible Leak," Monkey, along with a wolf, a tiger, and a thief, learn a lesson about truth and false fears.

Uchida, Yoshiko. *The Magic Listening Cap: More Folk Tales from Japan*. Berkeley: Creative Arts Books, 1987.

Monkey Folklore

Magic Animals of Japan tells some interesting folklore about monkeys in Japan, including how the Year of the Monkey began. It also has a different version of "Raw Monkey Liver."

Pratt, Davis. *Magic Animals of Japan*. Berkeley: Parnassus Press, 1967.

Japanese Macaque Distribution

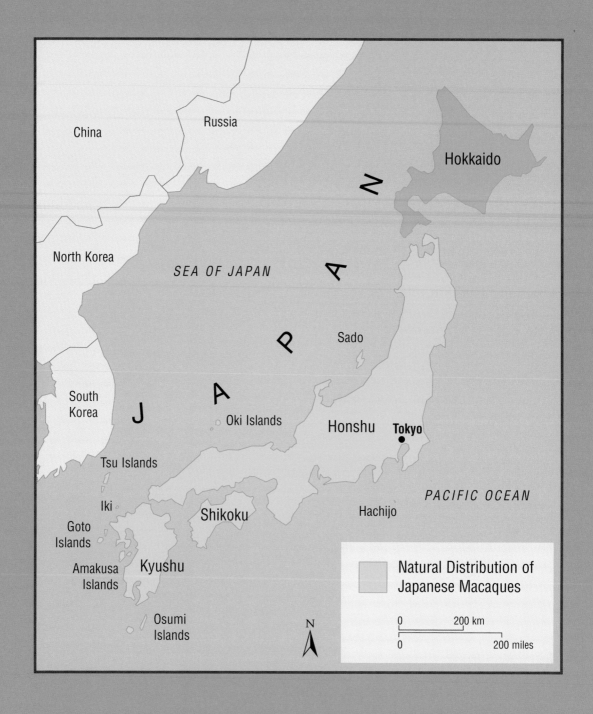

China

Russia

Hokkaido

North Korea

SEA OF JAPAN

N

Sado

South
Korea

J

A

P

A

Oki Islands

Honshu

Tokyo

Tsu Islands

PACIFIC OCEAN

Iki

Shikoku

Hachijo

Goto
Islands

Amakusa
Islands

Kyushu

Osumi
Islands

N

Natural Distribution of
Japanese Macaques

0   200 km

0   200 miles

Status

It is thought that there could be up to 100,000 macaques living in troops across Japan.

Opposite: Japanese macaques live on all of the Japanese islands except Hokkaido.

Scientists do not know the true population of Japanese macaques. The guesstimates that are given do not give the whole picture. Some areas are changing primarily because of factors that affect the life and health of the population. These factors include food, habitat, and human interference. It is thought that there could be up to 100,000 macaques living in troops across Japan, but it would be very difficult to prove that figure at this time. Some areas have a growing population, while populations in other areas are shrinking.

The Japanese macaque has been protected by the Japanese government since 1948. At that time, laws were passed banning its export, capture, or killing. This does not mean the animals are safe.

In areas where macaques raid crops, they may be classified as pests. The government can give permits for pest animals to be killed or captured. If this continues, many populations may disappear, and surviving populations may become increasingly unhealthy.

Forced to live in smaller areas, Japanese macaques must either starve or move into farming areas where they become pests. If there is no room for Japanese macaques, the world will lose a unique primate.

Habitat Loss

Loss of habitat is the biggest threat to the survival of wild Japanese macaques. The monkeys' habitat has been shrinking since the end of World War II. At that time the Japanese government decided to build up the forest industry. Huge areas of forest were clear cut and replanted with cedar trees that do not provide food for the macaques. Today these planted forests make up almost 50 percent of the forests in Japan. In some areas they make up nearly 70 percent, leaving little area for the macaques to live.

Natural forests have also been cut to make way for growing towns and cities. Farmland has also increased, reducing the available monkey habitat further. Even isolated areas are being developed into recreation sites such as ski resorts. Roads built to link resorts and cities cut through more monkey habitat. The macaques in many of these areas have no place to go.

Some Japanese macaques move into towns searching for food and space. Although some people may feed them, the monkeys usually wear out their welcome as they move into gardens and parks.

Many macaques are killed or trapped each year because of their crop-raiding activities.

Monkey Pests

The Japanese macaques were once believed to be protectors of children. Now many people believe them to be pests. So much macaque habitat has been destroyed that the monkeys have few places left to go. Hungry monkeys searching for food raid crops and gardens. Sometimes they spoil a whole harvest. They enter towns and cause damage. Sometimes they even bite people.

The farmers try to get rid of the monkeys by trapping or shooting them. Professional monkey hunters kill hundreds of monkeys each year. Some of the monkeys that are trapped are moved to other areas. The fate of many others is not known.

The Japanese government now has a program to put up electric fences to keep the monkeys away from crops. Still, the fences will not solve the problem of what the monkeys will eat or where they will go.

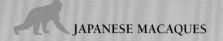
Viewpoints

Should scientists provision wild troops of Japanese macaques?

Since the early 1950s, many Japanese researchers have set out food for the monkey troops they were studying. Sometimes this was done to bring them into an open area where they could be easily watched. Sometimes it was done to see how they reacted to new foods or situations. Sometimes it was done to keep them from raiding farmers' fields. Many scientists wonder now whether this is a good idea.

PRO

CON

PRO

1 Many fascinating discoveries have come from studies of these monkeys. We can continue to learn about monkey behavior by studying these troops.

2 By providing food, scientists keep hungry monkeys from going into farmers' fields to raid crops.

3 By showing the Japanese people how special their monkeys are in monkey parks where food is supplied, people may care more about saving them.

CON

1 Provisioning is changing the macaques' natural behavior. Scientists should learn about the monkeys' natural behavior in their wild habitat before it all disappears.

2 Feeding causes troop sizes to become much larger. Eventually some may raid crops as they become used to human food.

3 Some monkeys are becoming aggressive toward people. They are entering homes and towns expecting handouts of food.

Snow Monkeys in Texas

One way you can help Japanese macaques is to support organizations that are working for them. A very interesting project is the Texas Snow Monkey Sanctuary.

In 1966 a large troop of Japanese macaques that was being provisioned by Japanese scientists divided into two groups. One of the groups became serious pests in a nearby town. In an effort to keep the monkeys from being destroyed, the scientists tried to find a new home for them.

In 1972 the entire troop was shipped to the United States. The troop was moved onto fenced ranch land in southern Texas. The monkeys were to be studied and provided with food. However, they lived in conditions that were as close to natural as possible. They had to learn to forage for new foods, avoid new predators, and handle a huge change in climate. They adapted remarkably well.

Now, over 25 years later, the Texas Snow Monkey Sanctuary is home to several hundred Japanese macaques. Many scientists come to the sanctuary to study the macaques every year. The sanctuary also provides a home for unwanted macaques from zoos and labs.

The sanctuary is a nonprofit organization. They accept donations to help care for the monkeys. Those who support the sanctuary are provided with a newsletter about the monkey troop.

No longer strangers, these Japanese macaques are at home in the hot, semi-arid Texas scrubland. The troop is thriving, and scientists have new chances to learn how adaptable the monkeys really are.

What You Can Do

Japanese macaques are fascinating animals that need our help. You can learn more about them by joining or writing to a conservation organization for more information.

Conservation Groups

INTERNATIONAL
World Wide Fund For Nature
Avenue du Mont Blanc
CH-1196 Gland,
Switzerland

International Primate Protection League
P.O. Box 766
Summerville, SC
29484
USA

The Primate Society of Japan
c/o Kyoto University
Primate Research Institute
Inuyama, Aichi 484
Japan

UNITED STATES
World Wildlife Fund United States
1250 24 Street NW
Washington, DC
20037

International Wildlife Coalition
70 East Falmouth Highway
East Falmouth, MA
02356

American Society of Primatologists
c/o Regional Primate
Research Center
University of Washington
Box 357330
Seattle, WA
98195

The Texas Snow Monkey Sanctuary
Dept. A
P.O. Box 702
Dilley, TX
78017

CANADA
World Wildlife Fund Canada
90 Eglington Avenue E,
Suite 504
Toronto, ON
M4P 2Z7

Twenty Fascinating Facts

1 A troop of Japanese macaques in Texas has a special warning call for rattlesnakes. They do not give the call for any other kind of animal, not even other snakes.

2 You can usually spot a dominant monkey by the behavior of other monkeys around it. They will move out of the dominant animal's way and will make a fear grimace.

3 In some species of macaques, stronger monkeys sometimes make weaker ones empty their cheek pouches and hand over the food.

4 The faces of newborn Japanese macaques are bright red. The color fades to pink by the second day.

5 The pigtailed macaque, a close relative of the Japanese macaque, has been trained to pick coconuts by farmers in Thailand. Their trainers pay them with bananas.

6 Japanese macaques usually sleep sitting upright in trees.

7 Among Japanese macaques, young females are the most likely to pick up and pass on new ideas or behaviors. Adult males are the least likely to learn them.

8 A group of Japanese macaques escaped from a zoo in northern Ontario, Canada, in 1988. Most of them were rounded up within a few days. The leader, however, stayed out for two weeks and often visited the local pizza parlor looking for food.

9 When Japanese macaques sit in a hot pool on a wintery day, the temperature of the water can be more than 100° F (60° C) warmer than the air above their heads.

10 Different troops of macaques sometimes have strong food preferences. The favorite food of one may be disliked and avoided by another.

11 Grooming helps maintain social bonds between macaques. Eating insects found in fur provides extra nutrition.

12 Japanese macaques began using the mountain hot springs in 1963 when a young female went into a hot spring where soybeans had been scattered. Others followed her example. Soon the whole troop was using the hot springs to warm their winter days.

13 Young Japanese macaques watch what their mothers are eating, then sniff their mother's mouths as if trying to remember the scent of the food.

14 An infant macaque's dark fur is a signal to adults that it deserves special treatment. Infants can get away with behavior no adult could.

15 Macaques sometimes walk upright on two legs when carrying objects.

16 Infant Japanese macaques are often introduced to water by clinging to their mothers' backs when they go swimming.

17 Very little interaction with predators has been seen among Japanese macaques. However, when a bobcat grabbed an infant in Texas, it was chased and mobbed by the whole troop.

18 Dozens of studies have been done on Japanese macaques in Japan. However, only one long-term study has been done on monkeys that have not been provisioned with food. This is on the island of Yakushima, the southernmost place these macaques live.

19 The Japanese word for monkey is "saru." This word also means "to go away." Traditionally monkeys have not been welcome at weddings for fear that they may make the bride run away.

20 Japanese macaques have been spotted using their opposable thumbs to make snowballs. They create small balls in their hands and then roll them on the ground to make larger balls, just as humans do.

Glossary

adaptable: Able to change to fit different conditions

dominance: A form of social power and influence

dominance hierarchies: Occur when there are regular, predictable dominance relationships in a group

feral: A domestic animal that has become wild

gestation: The length of time that a female is pregnant

home range: The entire area in which an animal lives

hormones: Chemicals made by certain glands in the body

matriline: A group of female monkeys who are all related

omnivore: An animal that eats both animal and plant foods

opposable: The ability to place either the first finger and thumb, or the big and second toes together to grasp things

peripheral males: Male monkeys that live on the edge of the troop and are low in the dominance hierarchy

primate: A member of a large order of animals that includes prosimians, monkeys, apes, and humans

provisioned: A group of animals that are provided with a steady supply of food by researchers

vocalizations: Sounds made to send messages to others or that express emotions

weaned: When a young animal does not drink milk from its mother anymore

Suggested Reading

Fedigan, Linda. *Primate Paradigms*. Montreal: Eden Press, 1982.

Fedigan, L.M., and J. Asquith (eds.). *The Monkeys of Arashiyama*. Albany: State University of New York Press, 1991.

Pavelka, Mary McDonald. *Monkeys of the Mesquite: The Social Life of the South Texas Snow Monkey*. Dubuque, Iowa: Kendall/Hunt Pub., 1993.

Overbeck, Cynthia. *Monkeys: The Japanese Macaques*. Minneapolis: Lerner Pub. Co., 1981.

Rau, Margaret. *The Snow Monkey at Home*. New York: Alfred A. Knopf, 1979.

SUGGESTED VIEWING

Mozu the Snow Monkey. Nature; 60 Minute Video, 1997.

MACAQUES ON THE INTERNET

One of the places you can find out more about Japanese macaques is on the Internet. Visit the following sites, or try searching on your own:

Animal Diversity
http://animaldiversity.ummz.umich.edu/accounts/macaca/m._fuscata.html

Mindy's Memory Monkey Facts
http://www.mindysmem.org/macaque.html

The Texas Snow Monkey Sanctuary
http://www.members.tripod.com/pages_2

Index

alpha female 16, 17
alpha male 16, 17, 42

birth 25, 26, 27
body language 20, 21
breeding 11, 15, 21,
    24, 42

cheek pouches 13, 28,
    39, 59
classification 8
competition 41-45

dominance hierarchies
    17

fear grimace 21, 59
feet 12, 26, 28
folklore 47-49
folktales 50–51
food 9, 10, 12, 13, 15,
    16, 25, 28, 29, 31,
    32, 33, 35, 37-39, 41,
    42, 45, 49, 53, 54,
    55, 56, 57, 59, 60, 61
forest 7, 10, 13, 31, 32,
    43, 44, 45, 54
fur 10, 11, 12, 26, 27,
    28, 33, 39, 41, 49,
    60, 61

grooming 18, 21, 27,
    39, 49, 60

habitat 7, 9, 12, 31-35,
    37, 39, 41, 42, 43,
    44, 45, 53, 54, 55, 56
hands 12, 26, 27, 28
hearing 13
home range 32, 33, 42

infants 16, 19, 23, 24,
    25, 26, 27, 28, 29,
    35, 38, 43, 61

juveniles 16, 19, 23,
    27, 29

life span 9

matriline 16, 17, 42
mountain 7, 9, 10, 31,
    43, 44, 60

nursing group 23, 28

peripheral male 17, 29
play 19, 21, 27, 28, 29
population 35, 45, 53
predator 9, 15, 20, 41,
    57, 61

primate 5, 7, 8, 12, 34,
    35, 53, 58
provisioning 16, 56,
    57, 61

seasonal activities 33
sight 13, 39
size 9, 29
skin 11, 18
smell 13, 39
status 53-57

teeth 13, 21, 39
Texas 5, 20, 35, 57, 58,
    59, 61
tree shaking display 21,
    32
troop 15, 16, 17, 18,
    19, 21, 23, 24, 25,
    27, 29, 32, 33, 34,
    35, 38, 41, 42, 49,
    53, 56, 57, 59, 60, 61

vocalizations 20, 21

weight 8, 9, 28